Muhammad Ali

by Jonatha A. Brown

Reading consultant: Susan Nations, M.Ed., author/literacy coach/consultant

WEEKLY READER

EARLY LEARNING LIBRARY™

Please visit our web site at: www.earlyliteracy.cc
For a free color catalog describing Weekly Reader® Early Learning Library's list
of high-quality books, call 1-877-445-5824 (USA) or 1-800-387-3178 (Canada).
Weekly Reader® Early Learning Library's fax: (414) 336-0164.

Library of Congress Cataloging-in-Publication Data

Brown, Jonatha A.
    Muhammad Ali / by Jonatha A. Brown.
      p. cm. — (People we should know)
    Includes bibliographical references and index.
    ISBN 0-8368-4743-1 (lib. bdg.)
    ISBN 0-8368-4750-4 (softcover)
    1. Ali, Muhammad, 1942-—Juvenile literature. 2. Boxers (Sports)—
United States—Biography—Juvenile literature. I. Title.
    GV1132.A4B76 2005
    796.83'092—dc22
    [B]   2004066126

This edition first published in 2006 by
Weekly Reader® Early Learning Library
A Member of the WRC Media Family of Companies
330 West Olive Street, Suite 100
Milwaukee, WI 53212 USA

Copyright © 2006 by Weekly Reader® Early Learning Library

Based on *Muhammad Ali* (Trailblazers of the Modern World series) by James Buckley Jr.
Editor: JoAnn Early Macken
Designer: Scott M. Krall
Picture researcher: Diane Laska-Swanke

Photo credits: Cover, title, pp. 10, 16, 19, 21 © AP/Wide World Photos; p. 5 © MPI/Getty Images;
p. 6 © The Courier-Journal; p. 9 © Kent Gavin/Keystone/Getty Images; p. 12 © Keystone/Getty
Images; p. 14 © Herb Scharfman/Time & Life Pictures/Getty Images; p. 15 © Express/Getty Images;
p. 17 © Dirck Halstead/Getty Images; p. 20 © Michael Cooper/Getty Images

Printed in the United States of America

1 2 3 4 5 6 7 8 9 09 08 07 06 05

Table of Contents

Words that appear in the glossary are printed in **boldface**
type the first time they occur in the text.

Chapter 1: Growing Up Black

Cassius Clay was born on January 17, 1942. His mother was a maid. His father was a sign painter. They did not have much money. They must have dreamed of a better life for their son, but they did not know he would one day become the great Muhammad Ali.

The Clays lived in Louisville, Kentucky. Back then, the city was split into two parts. One was for white people. The other was for black people. The white part of town was much nicer. White people had better jobs and more money. They ran the government. Black people did not like this system, but they were stuck with it.

The Clays were African Americans. They had dark skin. They lived in the poor part of Louisville. Mean

When Cassius was growing up in Louisville, black people lived in a poor part of town.

white children sometimes called Cassius names because he was black. This happened to many black boys and girls. They knew enough to keep quiet. If they talked back to a white person, there could be real trouble. Older whites might hurt them and their families. They did not want that to happen.

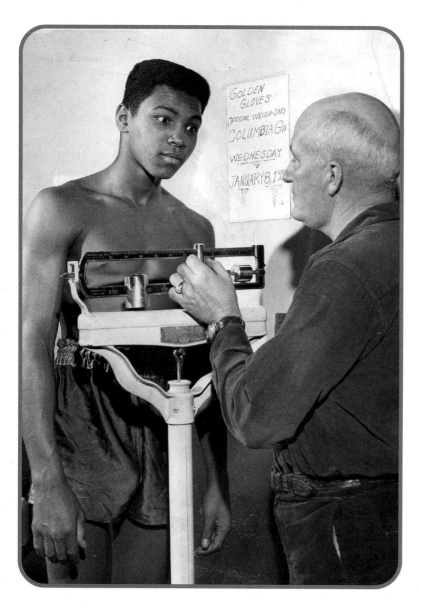

Joe Martin taught
young Cassius to box.

So they did not stand up
for themselves.

Learning the Ropes

When Cassius was twelve
years old, he met a white
man named Joe Martin.
Joe taught kids to box.
He did not care about the
color of their skin. He asked
if Cassius would like to
learn. The boy said yes.

He had plenty of natural
skill. He was a fast learner,
too. Soon he became quick
on his feet and could duck
away from a punch. He won
most of his matches. Then

he started boxing on a local TV show. Over the next few years, he won many state and national titles.

As a boxer, Cassius stood out because he was so good. He stood out in another way, too. Most black **athletes** did not talk much in public. They did not dare. White people might get mad at them. But Cassius was not quiet. He was loud. He **boasted** about his skill and made up funny little poems about his fights. Many people liked his colorful ways. And he liked the attention he got in return.

Golden Gloves

When he was a young man, Cassius Clay won the Golden Gloves, a tournament for boxers under eighteen. Many other top fighters have gotten their start winning this tounament!

Chapter 2: Olympic Champion

In 1960, Cassius was eighteen years old. That year, he earned a spot on the U.S. Olympic Team. It was an exciting time.

At the Games

There was only one problem. The Olympic Games were being held in Rome, Italy. Cassius would have to fly there in a plane. He had never flown before, and he was afraid. He did not want to get on the plane. Joe had to calm him down and help him face his fear. Finally, he got on the plane.

After Cassius got to Rome, he felt much better. He had some tough matches, but he won them all. When the games were over, he brought home a gold medal!

Cassius often clowned around and bragged about his skill.

He was very proud of his medal. He wore it all the time, even when he went to bed. He felt like a hero. He thought he had earned the respect of both black and white people.

A Homecoming Surprise

Cassius soon learned that little had changed in Louisville. He and some friends went to a diner to eat. The white owner did not want black people to eat there. He refused to serve them. Cassius was very angry. He felt hurt, too. Even though he had

In 1996, Ali was given a new Olympic gold medal to replace the one he threw away. Here, he is kissing his new medal.

won an Olympic gold medal, white people could still push him around. They could do this just because of the color of his skin. It was not fair.

Suddenly, he did not like his gold medal at all. He was still a black man in a white man's world. Filled with hurt, he threw his medal into a river! He felt that he would never really fit into the white man's world.

A Different Fight

A professional boxing match can take eight to fifteen rounds before it is finished. But Olympic boxing matches last only three rounds. These matches are judged on the number of punches each boxer lands. Special boxing gloves with white panels over the knuckles are also used in the Olympics.

Chapter 3: Fighting as a Hero

Angelo Dundee helped Cassius become the World Heavyweight Champion.

Cassius kept on boxing. In the past, he had earned prizes when he won fights. Now he earned money. He was a **professional**. It was time for him to hire a new trainer.

Going Pro

Angelo Dundee became Cassius Clay's trainer. Working with Angelo, Cassius won many matches. Each win seemed to give him more to boast about. His fans laughed at his funny poems. They liked his spirit and his skill in the ring.

Cassius began fighting the best **pros** he could find. Each match brought him closer to the greatest match of all. This was the fight for the World Heavyweight Championship.

Becoming the Greatest

The year was 1964. Sonny Liston was the World Heavyweight **Champion**. He had fought the best and won. He did not need to fight this bold young man to prove his skill. Yet Cassius kept saying he could beat him. Finally, Liston agreed to a match.

Most boxing fans thought Liston would win. When the fight started, they were surprised. Cassius was so fast that Liston could not hit him. Liston got tired. In the end, Cassius won! He was the new World Heavyweight Champion!

Cassius jumped up and down. He yelled, "I am the greatest! I am the greatest!" It was a big, big day for the young man.

A New Name

The next day, Cassius surprised people again. He told the world that he had become a **Muslim**. He had taken a new name, too. From now on, his name would be Muhammad Ali. Muhammad means "one worthy of praise."

Cassius was over-joyed when he beat Liston in 1964.

Fans were shocked. Some Americans did not know what a Muslim was. They did not know that Muslims practice Islam. This is an old and respected faith that is common in much of the world. Yet it was not well known in the United States.

Many white Americans turned against Ali. They did not like his new name. They were afraid of his new faith. Some said he hated his country. Some said he hated white people. In return, they did not like him.

Now a Muslim, Ali (second from right) took his new faith very seriously.

In other parts of the world, Ali was seen as a hero. He visited Africa, and crowds of people turned out to greet him. Most of them were both black and Muslim. They were proud of him.

Meanwhile, he kept boxing. He beat one great fighter after another. People could not deny that he was the best.

Fighting the Government

In 1967, Ali lost his boxing title. He did not lose it while fighting in the ring. A problem started when the U.S. government tried to make him join the army. He did not want to be a soldier. He said his faith did not allow him to fight in a war. He went to court and talked to a judge. The judge said he must go into the army. When he refused again, the judge said he was breaking the law. Because of this, the World Boxing Association took his title away. He was no longer the World Heavyweight Champion.

Ali was led away by officials after he refused to join the U.S. Army.

Ali could not box for more than three years. Finally, a judge said he could fight again. He came back strong and went after the new champion. But he had been away too long. He fought well, but the other man beat him. Ali was disappointed.

Soon after that, the courts changed their views about Ali and the army. They said his faith was a good reason for him not to join the army. He had not been breaking the law when he refused to join. His fans were happy to hear this. They hoped he would train hard now. They hoped he would win the World Heavyweight Championship again.

Ali won the World Heavyweight title a third time when he beat Leon Spinks in 1978.

Making a Comeback

Ali did train hard. He did win the title again. Yet it did not come easily. He had to work for years to get back on top. Then, in 1974, he beat the current champion. Again he could claim, "I am the greatest!" and few could disagree.

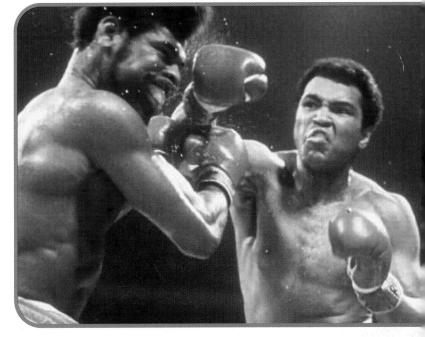

He held his title for four years. Then he lost a match to Leon Spinks. Just a few months later, they met in

the ring again. This time Ali won. He became
the only man ever to win the World Heavyweight
Championship three times!

Famous Words

Ali loved to tell people how great he was. When he
talked about his style in the ring, he often said, "Float
like a butterfly, sting like a bee." His fans loved to
hear him say those lines. They also liked to hear him
recite the many poems he made up about fighting
and his opponents. One of his most famous poems
was about Smokin' Joe Frazier.

I'll be pickin' and pokin'
Pouring water on his smokin'
This might shock and amaze ya
But I'm gonna destroy Joe Frazier.

Chapter 4: Helping Others

Ali retired from boxing in 1979. Five years later, his hands started to shake. He had **Parkinson's syndrome**. Doctors said it would get worse. Walking would become hard for him. He would have trouble talking, too. This was not good news. Even so, he did not let it stop him.

After retiring from boxing, Ali visited orphans in Africa in 1997.

He was now known all over the world. People loved and respected him. When he spoke, they listened. He decided to use his fame to spread a message of peace and love.

Changing the World

Ali's body did not work quite right, but he had a new job to do. He began traveling around the world.

The world cheered as Ali lit the Olympic flame at the 1996 Summer Games.

At each stop, he spoke about the need for peace. He asked people to try harder to understand others. He said that differences between people do not have to be scary or bad. People listened to his words and were moved by them.

Years have passed since then. Ali has worked for many good causes. He has helped to feed the hungry. He has worked with children who need a hero and a guiding hand.

He has helped people see that most Muslims are good people who care about others.

Ali has trouble moving these days. He does not spend as much time with his fans as he would like. But he still does all he can to help people in need. He is known everywhere as a truly great man.

In 1998, Ali founded the Muhammad Ali Center in Louisville, Kentucky. Its purpose is to encourage peace and understanding among all people.

Glossary

athletes — people who play sports

boasted — bragged

champion — winner

Muslim — a person who practices the faith of Islam

Parkinson's syndrome — an illness that makes it harder and harder for a person to move as time goes on

pro, professional — someone who plays a sport to make money

For More Information

Books

The Champ. Tonya Bolden (Knopf)

I Am Muslim. Religions of the World (series). Jessica Chalfonte
  (PowerKids Press)

I Shook Up the World: The Incredible Life of Muhammad Ali.
  Maryum Ali (Gareth Stevens)

The Story of Muhammad Ali. Leslie Garrett (DK Publishing)

Web Sites

How to Celebrate the Life of Muhammad Ali

www.ehow.com/how_14890_celebrate-life-muhammad.html
Ideas for people who care about Ali and his good works

Sports Illustrated Magazine Covers

*sportsillustrated.cnn.com/centurys_best/boxing/gallery/ali/
main/index.html*
Thirty-five magazine covers that show Ali through the years

Index

About the Author

Jonatha A. Brown has written several books for children. She lives in Phoenix, Arizona, with her husband and two dogs. If you happen to come by when she isn't at home working on a book, she's probably out riding or visiting with one of her horses. She may be gone for quite a while, so you'd better come back later.